IN YOUR SMALLEST POCKET

You'll find the unexpected

JANE O'SHEA

ISBN- 978-0-473-55458-3

Cover design by: Jess Le Marchand

www.wordremedies.co.nz

To Peter, Briar, Meg and Jess
I know where I belong

PREFACE

One day, not writing this book became more painful than my fear of writing it.

So I grabbed some chocolate, and other suitable distractions. A bit more chocolate, and I was ready to go.

Ten years after my first book.

TABLE OF CONTENTS

INTRODUCTION

It starts at the place where everything changes. That was when I almost died. It wasn't the almost dying that changed everything, it was what happened next.

I was at my brother's wedding, so I didn't want to make a fuss. My old 'friend' asthma had made a reappearance in my life, but with three wee children under four, dealing with it hadn't hit the urgent list. On this occasion, my breathing difficulties were making a particularly strong comeback. I thought I'd quietly slip outside, hide behind a tree, and try to get my breathing to behave itself.

Just as well my aunt-the-nurse came out to find me, because I don't remember anything until I realised that I was in an ambulance on my way to hospital. So much for not making a fuss…

The next week, I was sitting in front of my doctor, resisting all his attempts to put me on daily medication. With some compromising, we managed to negotiate a safe way for me to explore other options to get myself well. Mind you, I had no idea what those options might be.

First up, I thought I would do some research. Among other causes, there appeared to be some evidence that there was an emotional component to this asthma thing. This was tugging at my interest. Just like that one phrase in a song that gets stuck in your head ... emotional component, emotional component, emo ... The more I thought about it, the more uncomfortable I became. Meanwhile the invisible beast was still squeezing the breath right out of me.

Finally, the earworm won. If the asthma had any kind of emotional basis, what might it be? This turned out to be a smallish question with a biggish answer.

Once I let my guard down, it was game-on. There were clear signs that all was not well. I was stressed and precariously close to being overwhelmed. Riddled with self-doubt, I was constantly unkind to myself. And if I hadn't got sick, I might have stayed that way for the rest of my life. Or maybe something else would have broken under the strain of holding myself together.

This getting-myself-well business was a much bigger job than I had imagined, and I was pretty lost. So I did what I always do when I'm stuck: I made a plan. I decided to try everything and anything until I found what worked.

If I'd known how much time it would take and how much it would cost, I might have gone for the drugs. As it happened, I learned two things about healing: it follows a wobbly line, and it takes as long as it takes.

Just letting you know

I have written about the sexual abuse that happened to me as a child. It was a definite decision to include this part of myself and my writing. It felt disingenuous to keep this part of myself hidden. But more than that - if I let fear or judgment keep me quiet, then it would feel like I'd become part of the problem.

The chapter called 'Playing Hide and Seek' is about childhood trauma. The stories 'Some kind of murky grey' and 'It was done' also touch on this subject.

I'M LOVINGLY CAUGHT

(Coming home to yourself)

SURRENDERED
ALMOST FORGOTTEN
IT IS FOR ME
MY OWN MADE EARTH
JUST NOW
AMBUSHED
SAVED
WHAT REMAINS
JANE O'SHEA AND DISASSOCIATES

SURRENDERED

My tea cools down beside me
as I sit down to stress

I watch the wind dance through the long grass
which needs mowing since last I looked
The washing drying in the breeze
as the sun strolls from cloud to cloud

All around me
life is happening without effort
And here I am
in the middle
incessantly trying
struggling with this
urgency about that

Overlooking the uncomplicated fact
that life is already happening

Foolishness still prevails
as I try not to try

ALMOST FORGOTTEN

Tucked away in a corner
behind the have-tos and the everyday
are the ideals and ideas we once held so close

Now and then
we need to go in
and have a good rummage
to remember what's still important
Don't wait for the crisis

It's already getting late

All that was put away for later
in those safe
almost forgotten places
Time to make sure nothing
is left out or left behind

IT IS FOR ME

From its winter freeze
the icy heart-melt begins
and love starts to flow

Fresh new water
pours from the lonely mountains
down through the quiet valleys
moving over warming rocks and rich earth

Winding through the plains
warmed in the sun
curling its way here
to awaken my body
and bathe my aching heart

And to my surprise
this spring flood
of utterly tender love
is not for another
It is for me

MY OWN MADE EARTH

There is one place I like the best
A place that most people
would never guess

It's here
with my hands
deep in my compost bins
All four of them
large and in a row

Full to the brim with waste and scraps
seaweed, weeds, horse poo
and grounds from my local coffee house

Musty smell of rotting
feeding the worms and the microbes
The damp warmth
and rich dark brown finery
of my own made earth

Then lugged and dug into the garden beds
for the vegetables, for the flowers
for my sheer delighted pleasure

JUST NOW

Just now
I finally found enough quiet
to not have to engage
with this urgent and important world

The bone-cold and windless winter-still
drove me inwards
and I was able to hear once more
that sweet and faithful voice

'This small, shy inner-world still wants you'

That was enough
Just enough
To claim my life back
Just now

AMBUSHED

The mid-life-type crisis arrives
Unannounced
Inconvenient

An ambush

All those whispered
I'll do it one day's start to shout
The routines begin to weep
and the foundations shudder

Gripping tight, still holding on
we smile through our exhaustion
still hoping it will not happen

But the cracks keep exposing
and the shaking still threatens

The old stories can no longer
patch our life together

It's time to go down
to what is left undone
Begin to dismantle
all that we thought was so important

We don't yet know how
but we most definitely know
what we must do

SAVED

But nobody, nothing saved me

I had to plan and execute
the whole manoeuvre
by myself
It was clumsy and inefficient

But I got away, anyway

I did leave it till the very last minute
still hoping for a piece-of-cake escape

Willing rescuers aren't as common
as the storybooks proclaim

At large
Released
Unhinged perhaps

But free

WHAT REMAINS

I stubbornly spurned
what the world tried to make me
tried to make me believe

As quietly as possible
I didn't want to make a fuss

I almost doubted myself
into a graveyard of conformity
But the grandmothers
soothed and scolded from their crypts
pleading me on

I kicked and rebelled
inner mutiny often ensued
I retreated
but I always returned

I silently screamed and wept myself
inside out

Until I
was all that remained

I can still feel it - that sensation of being physically here, but essentially not. I didn't know there was any other way of feeling/being/existing. And when I finally worked it out, the worst part was realising that not only was I disassociated, I didn't have a clue how to reassociate.

This concept had popped up in reading that I'd been doing, so I knew about it in my head. I knew how to *think* about it. However I actually consciously *felt* it for the first time, when sitting with my best-and-most-useful-therapist. What made him the best and most useful, was that he would get me to be quiet, feel into my body, and to report what I'd discovered. Whereas the usual therapist trick of asking 20 questions never worked with me, because I could always come up with perfectly reasonable but utterly useless answers.

It was in one of our sessions that it occurred to me that I was, at that very moment, disassociated - just like the books had described. He did his best-and-most-useful-therapy and asked me to keep naming my experience. I told him, "It's like I'm living in a room, I can see and interact with the world through the windows, but I'm separate. I live in the room, and the rest of life is outside the room. I don't know how to find the door".

It then began to feel really shit-awful, as I realised that, not only did I not know how to get out of the room, I might not even want to. I had essentially traded feeling safe in exchange for being present. Interacting with the world straight-on felt distinctly dangerous.

So, the plan was to stay physically close to people as much as I could and notice what happened. My then-husband and I decided to try an experiment and tie ourselves together for a few days. We literally tied our ankles together. Going to the supermarket and having a pee were particularly hilarious. Other aspects were not so funny, as I felt my desperate need to get away, to disappear, to disengage. But it worked a treat as I shocked myself out of that room and into the present. I now knew what it felt like, and could pull myself back whenever I started to head towards that safe-but-lonely room.

I don't live in that room anymore, I don't even visit.

TRIPPING OVER MYSELF

(self-doubt and other dangerous things)

SUCH DANGEROUS THINGS

There is a wee hole
in the lattice of my wellbeing
That intricate lacy scaffolding
that keeps me upright and whole

And through such a tiny gap
can crawl
belly first
such dangerous things

Those daunting doubting winds
that whistle through
in the dark of night
leaving distrust and haunting suspicion

Those silent stinging comments
that leave raw, red welts of misgiving

And through these smallest of cracks
those wheedling roots of weedy thoughts
plant themselves in my heart
and grow furiously in the rain

FOR DEAR LIFE

Don't teach our children that
they can do anything, everything
Stop teaching them about success

Teach them instead how to take
care of themselves
amid this uncertain
change and turmoil

Teach them how to grieve
for the world that should
have been theirs
Before the climate changed
before life became even more
complicated

Teach them to be grateful
for each good thing
And to know how to distill
what still remains true
and to stay faithful

And most of all
teach them about failure
The acceptance of a battle lost
and the ability to keep going
in the face of sure defeat

Teach them how to hold on
to what is dear
And to hold on
for dear life

FOR MYSELF

I am not defined
by how others see me

The earth does not say
"the sun does not love me"
when its warmth is muted by the clouds

When autumn leaves cover the ground
the grass does not say
"I am no longer important"

The mamaku standing tall in the forest
does not wilt from lack of praise
It knows that it is grand
doesn't need to be told

I too
am defined
By myself
For myself

MY ORPHANED IMAGINATION

In truth
when I began
it was impossible
My longing was a dark fugitive
My imagination orphaned
in this grown-up world

With sincerity and resolve
I began to write
one right word and then another
One small act of self-rebellion at a time

From the dark shadows of my imagination
my words escaped
and found their way here
To this page

My words found their way home
to me
The writer

WHAT SHALL I BE

I asked my dad once
"What do you think I should do when I leave school"
"Whatever you want, dear"
I didn't know how to know what I wanted

I told my mother
"I think I'd like to go to broadcasting school"
"What makes you think you could do that"
I was so untested in my seventeen year old world
that I didn't know how to answer

I told my friend
"I think I'll be a teacher"
"You'd be lousy at that"
I didn't know enough to ask her how she knew

So I asked the guidance counsellor
for some guidance
"I think you should be a teacher"
I hit a confused dead end

I went to university and tried on a few things
Until I asked myself why
With no decent answer, I quit

So I put a pack on my back and hitch-hiked
my way through life, doing whatever found me
Mostly I enjoyed myself
Mostly it was good and I paid my way

Meanwhile, I asked an interested man
"What should I do with my life"
"Marry me, and come and live mine"
So I carefully, cunningly avoided the question
by living somebody else's life

But the question still sat there
"What to do when I grow up"
Then at last the answer found me
"That thing you have always longed for
that you believed you could never have"

TUCKED IN AN ENVELOPE

How do they do it
So self-assured
So decidedly confident
of their place in the world

So definite
that who they are
is good enough
That what they do
is enough

How do they keep
this unfailing belief
in themselves

Is it given out at birth
Do we inherit it from a great-aunt
win it in a raffle
or go buy it somewhere

I thought it might come with age
I might find it in a book
or in the vege garden

Someone might hand it to me
with my morning coffee
or tucked inside the envelope
with my birthday card

Through everything
self-doubt still hangs around
Ready to pounce
whenever I stumble

TUGBOAT

When I was small
I wanted to be
the tugboat skipper
or steer the pilot boat

Be something small that could
push big things around
Out there in the fresh empty air
lots of space and no people

It was a shame I got seasick
And a pity I was a girl

Where is the line between helpful and unhelpful? When does healthy become unhealthy - even toxic? I'm talking about the self-help industry. The first books I read were definitely helpful, giving me language to think and talk about stuff. The concepts and suggestions helped me to start to rearrange my self-image and overhaul some behaviours and habits. Mostly, the books showed me I wasn't alone, and maybe not so weird and flawed after all. A great start.

Therapy is a mixed bag. Some therapists do more harm than good. When I first started, I didn't know what signs to look out for. I've since learnt the clues. There are therapists who stir up stuff for its own sake, either without resolution or with very slow expensive progress. There are some who ask endless questions that lead nowhere. And there are therapists who give lots of sympathy and understanding, which leaves their clients feeling like victims - when strategies and encouragement would be more useful. In general, therapists have an intrinsic conflict of interest with getting their clients functional quickly. After all, I've never heard of a therapist giving a fixed quote.

Between the therapists, the books, and my own internal chatter, I was in danger of driving myself down the endless road of trying to fix myself with no 'fixed' address in sight. How long would I keep driving, looking out for some magic signpost pointing towards the finish? Not one book or therapist ever said, "Good job, good enough. Here are the strategies for when you get shaky - now off you go". What I got was lots of, "Well we'll need to have a deeper look into that".

It took a telling moment for me to twig to the game my then-husband and I were playing, and to call time. In the middle of an argument, he was once again pointing out what was wrong with me. This time I shot back "Why don't you write a list so I don't forget, and with priorities, so I fix the worst bits first. Or would you rather I have an entire personality transplant?"

It was then that this precious gem popped into my head… "Maybe the only thing broken about me is the belief that I'm broken". This was a very novel thought, because finding fault with myself was my favourite sport. I decided I needed a second opinion.

So I got one. I set up a lunch date with a darling-friend-the-friendly-psychologist and popped the question. His answer was chocolate mousse for my heart. "My dear Jane, I am so glad you have finally worked this out". As quick as a flash, I believed him. And once I believed him, I believed myself.

THIS COURTSHIP WITH ENOUGH

(being kind to ourselves)

THIS COURTSHIP WITH ENOUGH

I want to keep
my life right here
Grateful for all I have
wishing for nothing more

I don't want a life
any bigger than I have
I am content with this life
deep with naïve simplicity

I am loving
this calm
this quiet
Looking with soft eyes
and taking my time

This permission
I have given myself

This courtship with enough

OFF YOU GO

I want you to be kind
to yourself

No, not when
you're ready

Earlier than that

Off you go

BEING EQUALLY KIND

It's not easy to answer
when our instant, exhausting response
is invariably yes

Unwilling to disappoint
we never quite know who to help first

How to be kind to the other
and equally kind to ourselves

SMILING BACK

Being strong is not being a rock
hard and unbreakable

It's all the pieces left behind
when everything falls apart

It's loving the mirror and smiling back
accepting all the reflections
even when we don't know who we are anymore
even when we don't know what to do

Strength is a living membrane
responding to the moment
No longer arguing with what is

Bearing to stay in that place
of not knowing

THIS MORNING'S CHORUS

This morning's chorus
was a shambles
Each bird just going for it

No harmonising
no collaboration
no audience awareness
no attention to detail
no Facebook post, no selfies

Just an open-throated and full-bellied
desire to celebrate nothing more
than this day's dawning

My delighted morning ears
stirred my body
my dreamy night brain fell away
and a wee kiss good morning woke my heart

Having taken strict instructions
from the wayward birds
I rolled out of bed
oblivious to anything expected of me

WHEN I WAS YOUNGER

When I think how wired I was
how much energy was frittered away
on emotional angst and trying too hard

When I think of the waste
All that precious liveliness
taken for granted

How careful I have become
Kinder to myself and others
and grateful

MY VERY OWN IN-HOUSE BULLY

Most of my adult life, people have commented on how disciplined and driven I am. I have never believed them. I've got inside knowledge. I know the truth. I am not disciplined, I'm a bully. I bully myself. Any external critic or taskmaster has nothing on my in-house tyrant. I can harass and bully myself, all by myself.

Having a tidy house and having things neat, has got nothing to do with discipline and everything to do with keeping control. When things outside of me are untidy, I have trouble keeping my insides tidy. And when my insides are untidy, the scaffolding is in danger of toppling over. Then what will I do?

Constantly doing stuff doesn't mean that I am disciplined; it simply means that I am scared to stop. Scared that everything will pile up and I will be overwhelmed.

In the past, believing that I could only be loved if I was helpful and useful, was another mechanism that kept me in continual motion. My exaggerated attention to detail was nothing more than my fear of being discovered as incompetent.

I have an inflexible relationship with time for exactly the same reason. I like now. Now is safe and controllable. Now keeps me busy, so I don't have to worry about any kind of unkind future. Whereas my now-husband loves later. He throws everything into that safe and expansive future and believes that all will be well. Me, I hate later. Later means that all those unknown things might arrive at the same time and cause chaos - lawless, unruly, overwhelming.

As you might guess, husband and I have a completely different definition of soon. For me, soon arrives very closely after now. For husband, soon comes just before later. Uh-oh.

SO VERY BUSY BEING BUSY

(Slowing down)

THE SUN HAS STARTED SLEEPING IN

The yellow and orange sunflowers
have almost gone from my garden
Just a few brave blooms remain

A sighed relief
that summer has had enough
of rushing about
The sun has started sleeping in
letting the birds snooze
a little longer each morning

The cooling calm at dusk
holds a promise

The winter quiet is coming
curled up warm and snug at home
The wet and cold to keep me inside
The greying dark a reminder
that it's time for rest

SO BUSY BEING BUSY

It happened again

I fell into the great well of forgetting
lost in lists, demands and worry
Too busy being busy

I got caught up in the doing
and forgot what I was doing it for

Climbing up the ladder
only works if it is against the right wall
Ticking off the list
if it achieves something I still believe in
Finishing the plan
if I end up somewhere that matters

So very busy being busy

A SIMPLE LIFE

I've worked really hard for a simple life
Saying no is so unfashionable

Going up against the serious significance
the important busyness
of yes

Up to one's ears
in being successful

I thought that saying yes
would bring me a better
more interesting life

Turns out
just made me tired

WAITING

Current wisdom asserts
that we do not dawdle
That we take things head on
be brave, be determined, forge ahead

But sometimes
hiding
running away
or taking our time
is for the best

Until we are ready
to try again
To venture out
holding on to ourselves
No matter what we may find

Permission
to have a rest, recuperate
before we start out again
And only when we are ready

Taking all things
at our own sweet pace
to our own whispered place

LEFT WANTING

I see you striving
and wonder
where it all leads
So much devoted effort

I see you striving
and wonder
if this place called success
even exists

I see your wide-eyed expectation
of a life full to the brim
with achieving, with accomplishment
prosperity and promise

And I wonder
what will happen
when all the striving
leads to strife
And all the wanting
leaves you wanting

LULLABY FOR A GROWN UP

I have softened the lights
closed the doors
and pulled all the plugs

Rest your head right here
I have something to tell you

It's time to stop
You no longer need to believe
those damning and demanding voices
– your own or others'

Time to untangle the net
of every expanding choice

There is nothing for you
to do, to fix, to say, to decide

It's quiet
It's still
It is yours

QUIET NOW

I have no problem
with silence

Sometimes I wish the whole world
would shut-up

Including me

BEING A BUSY-BACK-SOON

How many times do I get asked the question, "Are you busy?", "Had a busy day?" or even simply, "Busy?" Asking about busyness has become a form of greeting much the same as "How are you?" Nobody expects an honest response. We are expected to say, "Yes", because being busy has become admirable.

I give them an honest response and it goes something like this. Either, "Unfortunately yes, which is not how I like to live my life", or, "No, I've worked really hard to un-busy my life and I like it like that".

People seem a little taken aback at first, then give a long sigh, get a faraway look in their eyes and say something like, "Oh, that would be nice", or "Good on you, I wish I could do that!"

What a bizarre notion we have about busyness. As if 'busy' means we are successful or important or popular. We seem to have swallowed the mantra and manuals from the nineties, urging us to manage time so we can be more efficient, more effective, and more productive. As if it's possible to manage time. We were never really told why, it was just vaguely hinted that we would be happier and/or richer.

Even our holidays must be jam-packed with activity – 'proof' that we are having a good time. The constant doing showing that we are immersing ourselves in another culture, or imbibing nature. Equally, we 'prove' that we are relaxing by doing yoga or meditation classes.

Bullied by endless lists, breathless with activity, busyness appears to have become the end goal.

A RUNAWAY MIND

(antics of the mind)

A RUNAWAY MIND

The problem with a runaway mind
is it leaves you brainless

Just when you need it to think something
your brains gone rouge
Just when you need to do something
There's nothing there

A runaway mind
tells you stories
that scare you senseless
Repeating reruns
with deadening regularity

A runaway mind
allows unwanted gatecrashers
to ruin your party
Conducting an entire chorus
of unhelpful advice

A runaway mind
is a pack of spooked horses
stampeding off in every direction

A runaway mind
is exhausting

LOSING MY MIND

I don't think
I've lost it
Not really lost it

I'm sure I put it down
around here
Someplace

I'm sure it's still
waiting for me
Somewhere

HELPING MYSELF FEEL BETTER

I'll have a trim latte
and a piece of cinnamon cake please

Would you like cream
or yoghurt with that

Both please

NOT TO WORRY

You don't need to worry
It hasn't happened yet

And if it does
you'll be too busy
dealing with it
to worry

THE PREVAILING QUESTION

It's the right questions
that change the world far more
than the right answers

Grabbing the limelight
answers are as proud as punch
Even when answering the wrong question

Even when answering the right question
self-important answers
believe in themselves perfectly
Forgetting that any answer is just for now

Answers argue, questions wait
Answers spin
questions know their place

Answers come and go
Questions endure

WHEN OUR HABITS BETRAY US

When our old habits betray us
best we find better friends
to help us on our way

Mr Will Power only works on good days
On a bad day
Mr Will Power won't get out of bed

Mrs Motivation is not always motivated
And being full of excuses
waxes and wanes and does as she pleases

However
may I introduce you to Constance Routine
an old and reliable friend

Ms Routine doesn't like sudden moves
takes things slow and steady
One small change before another

She is kind
always wanting the best for us
Constance Routine is most agreeable
always doing what she's asked

A HEAD FULL OF RERUNS

What a relief it would be to work out the mysteries of the mind. I was brought up to believe that the heart was illogical and irrational, and the mind was the sensible bit. Yet I constantly watch my mind gallop off in all directions; with distractions, ideas, excuses, plans, worries.

I rein it in, and in the wink of an eye, it's off again. Keeping track of it is exhausting, letting it run amok is disastrous. If I sit back and watch my mind without getting caught up in the story, it can actually be quite amusing.

The more I develop the discipline of watching, the more I catch myself ruminating on something, or having the same conversation over and over inside my head, or worrying and fretting about some future event.

It's horrifying to think that I used to believe all the crap that goes on in my head. And for a long time, I thought I was the only one with so much rubbish in there. But after years of working with others, I have come to realise that I am by no means the only one struggling with a runaway mind.

I've read that we have about 60,000 thoughts a day, and that 99.9% of them are the same thoughts we had yesterday, last year, a decade ago. What a waste of thinking! This amazing brain, littered with reruns.

I remember when I first realised that I could watch my mind. It meant there had to be another part of me doing the watching. I don't get invited to something, and away my mind goes - "nobody likes you, remember when blah blah blah". My husband does or doesn't do something - "See, he doesn't care about you. Just like when he …" and out comes the emotional filing cabinet with every slight and misdemeanour carefully filed for easy reference.

What a liberation to know that my mind isn't the only thing running the show. I can catch myself thinking an habitual unhelpful thought, and can choose to change it.

The trick is catching myself.

NOTHING LEFT TO THINK

(paying attention)

SWEET SILENCE
NOTHING LEFT TO THINK
SEEING PAST ME
SNEAKING UP ON MYSELF
I'D RATHER
EVEN MY MIND ESCAPES
ALWAYS THE THREAD
SIT WITH YOU
THE MOMENT I NOTICE
WITH JUST ONE BREATH
HAVING AN INSIDE

SWEET SILENCE

When the complaints
have talked themselves
into a tiresome stupor

When the old stories are bored
even with themselves
And blame can find no one to listen

When the drama has finally
played itself out

All that is left is stillness

The sweetest silence

NOTHING LEFT TO THINK

When I can't get my head straight
When I'm overthinking
When my thoughts disturb and interrupt

That's when I go to the beach
inhale the tiny drops of sea caught in the wind
watch the small pebbles dance with the waves
hear the low rumble of their teasing delight
taste the bite of salt on my lips
collect tiny pieces of polished glass

And then there is nothing left to think

That's when I go to the bush
Breath the air just breathed by the birds
watch the leaves playing with the wind
inhale that deep damp fragrance after rain

And then there is nothing left to think

That's when I go to my garden
Smile back at the flowers who are still smiling at the sun
bury my hands in the moist brown earth

And then there is nothing left to think

Sometimes I simply walk
one foot and then the other
Each step gently resting on solid ground

And then there is nothing left to think

SEEING PAST ME

There is nothing out there
Only me in here
looking out through masked eyes
perceiving, judging, interpreting

There is nothing out there
that is not seen by me in here

Imprinted on my eyes
are all the many things
I have seen before
Leaving their obscuring points and patterns

Only through curious and careful eyes
can I see past me
to the faintest, tiniest glimpse
of what might actually be out there

SNEAKING UP ON MYSELF

Everything I need
is right here

All I need do
is look a little closer
Creep around the corner
quietly
sneakily
and catch it quick

Before my wanting heart
my critical brain
my restless mind
takes over

I'D RATHER

I'd rather
look at the landscape at the beach
than a pretty picture on a wall
Walk in the park than through an art gallery
Enjoy it than Facebook it
Do it than watch it

I'd rather
play music badly
than listen to it expertly played
Eat what I've grown
than something fancy I can't pronounce
Make it than buy it

I'd rather
leave my phone behind and risk missing out
than take it with me, hoping
Miss a call than miss what's happening
Be with you than txt you

I'd rather
be by myself than try too hard to be with others
Get hurt than close my heart
Walk in the dark than be scared of it
Risk being embarrassed
than be compelled to prove I'm right

EVEN MY MIND ESCAPES

In the soft stillness of silent solitude
my heart overflows
into this soothing expanse

Billowing breaths touching everything
the greenness of a delicate fern
the quietness of the shadowing dawn
the endlessness of flowing water

And for these few moments
even my mind escapes

ALWAYS A THREAD

A fine line, a thread
weaving through our lives
Inherited strands from the ancestors
an umbilical cord from the past
Always a thread

A fragile silken filament
exquisitely embroidered on our hearts
Twisted and twirled into a thick rope
secured to the moorings

Knotted and tied into a hammock
rested and held
Sometimes a tangled net of frustration
Sometimes a string of lights in celebration

Always that thread
Intricately lacing
the earth to our bodies
our hearts to each other
to our spirit and beyond

Play with me, my friend
each of our threads
entwined and looped

Romp and leap with me
as we weave this blanket
of belonging
The very fabric of our lives

SIT WITH YOU

I can't help you
All I can do is point to
the prison in your mind

I can't heal you
Just remind you of
your once-trusting heart

I can sit with you
as you find your way back

Celebrate with you
as you devote yourself
to this moment

THE MOMENT I NOTICE

I never did find that purpose
By the time I stopped

it didn't matter anymore
The searching ended

the moment I noticed
But I kept walking

the soothing rhythm of my footfall
the steadying horizon

Noticing
Quietly attending

Finding my feet
on this crowded earth

WITH JUST ONE BREATH

I forgot to breathe
Not the dying kind of not-breathing

But the kind of not-breathing
that comes from distraction
Absent
ignoring where I am
neglecting what I'm doing

The kind of not-breathing
that happens when I'm too busy out-there
and lose touch with in-here

The kind of not-breathing
that opens the door
for anxiety and mistrust

Until the moment I notice
And with that awakening nudge
I'm back
Stirred from my unconsciousness
aware of myself in this place, now

With just that one breath
I am delivered back to here

HAVING AN INSIDE

When Daughter-Number-One was about eight years old, she came home from school one day, announcing that I was going to teach her class about Buddha. Seems they were studying a sister school in China, which happened to be Buddhist, and when one of the kids asked what Buddhism was, my daughter mentioned I had a statue of Buddha.

Sure enough, her teacher called me that night, extending the invitation to come and share what I knew about Buddhism. Though not believing that having a statue of Buddha gave me any right to talk about Buddhism, I still said yes.

Then I began to fret about how to explain the complexities of Buddhism to a class of eight year olds, when I barely understood it myself. I had this image of me standing up the front, clutching my wee statue, and boring them all to disruption. Best I could think of doing, was to give them an experience.

Before I knew it, there I was statue in hand, with 25 pairs of expectant eyes looking up at me, ready to make a risky start.

I asked them all to lie on the floor and close their eyes. I got sideways what-are-you-doing glares from my daughter, giggling from the girls, and smart-ass comments from the boys.

I pushed on, asking them to feel the weight of their bodies on the floor, the coldness of the air, their clothes on their skin, their hair on their heads. To notice the noises outside and the sound of my voice. Finally, to notice their breath coming in and going out.

To my great relief, they quietened down. I encouraged them to focus on their breathing and the sensations of their bodies. I even asked them to notice themselves thinking.

I didn't want to push my luck, so after about ten minutes I invited them to slowly open their eyes, sit up, and tell me what had happened.

One boy jumped up throwing his arms in the air, and proclaimed "I didn't know I had an inside!"

MY HURTING HEART WON'T LISTEN

(pain and heartache)

TRUSTING OUR WAY
THE PROMISE
LEFT BEREFT
A BITTER STAIN
MY HURTING HEART WON'T LISTEN
AVOIDING HEARTACHE
IN THE MIDDLE OF THE STREET
VULNERABLE

TRUSTING OUR WAY

On our way to closer friendship
sometimes we'll bang into each other
drop a word into an old wound
poke a finger into a tender spot

Reminder of what is still left
sore and awkward within us

The only thing we can do
is trust our way through the hurt
Step forward and soften
moving gracefully
through the conflict

Breathing and believing
the best in each other

THE PROMISE

When I committed to you
I promised to give it everything

I believed in that promise with all my heart

Now
as things fall apart
I must blame you
Otherwise my best wasn't good enough
Otherwise I can't trust my own heart

And if I allow that to be remotely true
where might that lead

Where might that lead

LEFT BEREFT

I should have known by his lazy touch
but I married him anyway

Forgetting to expect
I hoped instead

And when love didn't come
I was left bereft
But not surprised

A BITTER STAIN

Betrayal lives on the other side of truth
The thing not said
will forever be too late

Betrayal is not always in the deed
Betrayal is also in the secret
the cowardice of omission

With every denial
with each confessional moment lost
the wound of betrayal deepens
long before the truth is even known

Each lie
each truth withheld
leaves a bitter heart-stain
the shadow of which
takes a long time
to fade into forgiveness

MY HURTING HEART STILL WON'T LISTEN

I get a fright
I get scared
I become anxious and uncertain

Understanding is usually enough
but sometimes my head
can't convince my heart
to listen
or to trust

I fret
trying to remind myself
of all the love and goodness

But still my hurting heart
won't listen

AVOIDING HEARTACHE

I am desperately afraid of heartache

I want to control things
Watchfully anticipating
steeling myself
withdrawing
Wilfully determined

Interrupting the enjoyment of now
in a vain hope
that by being ready
I can avoid any kind of dreaded surprise

As if readiness ever stopped heartache
As if being forewarned
ever lessened the pain

IN THE MIDDLE OF THE STREET

It wasn't just the wheels that fell off
it was everything
And I was left there
sore and naked
in the middle of a busy street

There were too many
fast moving things
and I could not find
an unlocked door
a coat big enough
a manhole
or my wings

I just stood there
excruciatingly exposed

Nobody came
Maybe it was my own fault
but still
nobody came

VULNERABLE

Nobody told me that intimacy includes vulnerability. I thought that intimacy would come about when I was good enough to be loved.

When I felt vulnerable, I would hide myself. Pretend to be big and tough and strong, and hope nobody would notice. When I made a mistake or my behaviour was lacking, I'd cut myself off or hide myself away - once again hoping that nobody would notice. Of course, this gave me the opposite of what I really wanted, which was to be accepted and supported. Just when I needed help, I'd get all heroic. Just when I needed reassurance, I'd get grouchy and push people away, or go quiet and hide.

Even though it feels good to help others. Even though I feel open hearted when others need me. And even though I soften when people show me their doubts and fears, I struggle to believe that others have the same feelings for me.

It still takes me by surprise when people experience me differently from how I experience myself. Inside, I am as soft as cotton-wool, and know that my woolly stuffing could fall out at any moment. Others don't always notice.

I ran a retreat with guests, family, and friends constantly coming and going. I invented coping strategies to ensure that I didn't get overloaded. I would work consistently, always moving, getting through what needed to be done one task at a time, never rushing and never stopping. Quietly planning in advance, making sure everything ran smoothly and that I was on top of it all. I hated surprises and I hated pressure, so things were always done to plan and ahead of time.

In truth, I was but one hour or one item on my list away from being overwhelmed and everything turning to custard. I was the clichéd swimming swan - serene on the surface but paddling like crazy under the water.

An example was when we had some high-maintenance friends staying yet again. They increased my workload by making messes, wanting long conversations, asking for things, etc. Starting to feel resentful, I decided to ask them to be more considerate. They were gobsmacked. I was equally gobsmacked when I realised they had no idea of the pressure I felt when they stayed. They saw me as effortlessly efficient and calm.

There was a disconnect between how I felt on the inside and how I portrayed myself on the outside. It appears that my stoic and heroic façade worked extremely well and the vulnerable, overworked, any-minute-swamped me didn't show through.

This became apparent again a few weeks later. We were putting in a new sewage system and the whole of our front lawn was a dug-up mess. We had a team of people helping, and my then-husband was managing the project. On this particular day he assigned the only other female to do light work. He assigned me to move a pile of rocks. When I asked him about it, he said that she radiated a certain vulnerability and his response was to want to take care of her. When I asked him why he didn't have that response to me, he said "there is no room for me to take care of you, you are too busy taking care of yourself". Hmmffff!

As much as this stung, I knew he was right. I had been protecting myself for so long that I didn't know how to let anyone see what I needed, or that I needed at all. I longed for someone to take care of me, and at the same time I was too scared to let anyone see how vulnerable

I was. Pretty hard to blame those around me. Bugger, shit, bugger. This was all about me and I had no idea how to change it. That was until another conversation penetrated my stoic façade.

I had just left my husband, my retreat, my income, my home. I had softly landed at a friend's house, stunned, tired and determined. A dear friend who knows me well came to visit. He said, "Now Jane, for God's sake let your friends take care of you. I have seen you give and give and give, and it is time for you to receive. And by the way, that is not a compliment".

Someone had finally called my bluff. So I did just as he said. It really wasn't that hard. My friends looked after me beautifully. Nothing terrible happened. With their help, I got back on my feet in no time and was ready to build a new life.

PLAYING HIDE AND SEEK

(healing childhood trauma)

PLAYING HIDE AND SEEK WITH THE PAST
THE COURAGE TO SPEAK
WHEN YOUR STUFFING FALLS OUT
THE TRUTH ABOUT MYSELF
DON'T LET THEM WIN
WILDS OF THE LOST
ON WAKING
BEING LOST
A REAL LIFE BEGINS
NO MATTER
THE DEBRIS LEFT BEHIND

PLAYING HIDE AND SEEK WITH THE PAST

Today
those old memories
found me again
Tracking me down
and reminding me of
the long-buried past

I indulged in a few
of my favourite distractions
all the while knowing
they could not save me

I got lost
playing hide and seek
with the past

And finally
I had to admit
that I am still afraid
of those old cold ghosts

They can still reach through
from the past
and catch me

THE COURAGE TO SPEAK

Yes, I was hurt
A child, abused and alone

If I do not speak of it
If shame holds my tongue
then I remain complicit
and this quiet curse continues

Consent by silence
allows these wretched things
to happen
to still happen
to the young and tender

The first thing to be done
is to speak of it

So yes, I was hurt
A child, abused and alone

WHEN YOUR STUFFING FALLS OUT

When childhood knocks
the stuffing out of you

You look out
at the great picture of life
and can't see yourself

When you go off looking
for your place of belonging
and can't find yourself anywhere

Until the day
you find yourself
just where you were abandoned

And holding your own hand
you venture out to claim for yourself
that which had been stolen

THE TRUTH ABOUT MYSELF

I am already
all these good things
lovely, loveable, loving

Anything else I tell myself
is a lie

Every day I cleanse myself
not of any sin
but of the contaminating thought
that I am broken

I am waking from the delusion
that I am not good enough
that I am not enough

Talking back to those damaging voices
left raging inside my head

Looking into the mirror of my innocence
and seeing the sweet smile of relief
play on my face
and rest into my eyes

DON'T LET THEM WIN

Do whatever it takes to mend yourself
The childhood abuse, the neglect
it was not your fault

Don't let blame or shame
stop you from putting
yourself back together
From clearing away the debris
left behind

If you don't
If what happened then
tarnishes what happens now
Then they will have won
They will have won

WILDS OF THE LOST

When I take care of the wee hurt me
she slowly wanders back up the long path
emerging from the wilds of the lost

She is brave
to be both
expectant and afraid

I never quite know what to do

But I will not leave her
Not again
Not like everyone else
Not again
Not like that

ON WAKING

I went to sleep quite safe in my dreamy bed
trusting in an innocent and noble sleep
but awoke to a tangled mess

Right between my belly and my heart
wet rags of doubt
tossed about
Tied into clumps of foreboding
Touchy bundles of misgivings

Cheated of a replenishing sleep
I awoke diminished
In my deep sleepy rest
my defences had weakened
and the old stories had swarmed in

I so needed the beauty of that morning
to help me rearrange
myself back into the present

To choose again
the goodness of my grown up life

BEING LOST

I'm in and out of that door
The one leading into the world

Sitting on the doorstep
legs pulled up
leaning back against the door frame
I am neither in nor out

Scared of losing myself *in here*
Those old voices inside my head
still giving bad advice
The sickness in the pit of my belly
already ready to spread
Dreading those nauseating feelings
Scared of crumbling in on top of myself
Buried alive

Scared of *out there* too
Swamped
Never sure which way to go
Swept away
Vanishing into the crowding
Unbalanced by the constant and continual bustle
Clamouring

I sit in the doorframe
Scared of being lost in here
Scared of being lost out there

A REAL LIFE BEGINS

Being numb
is to be invisible
asleep to yourself and any kind of promise
Choosing to feel nothing
is sometimes the best you can do

Being afraid
is better than being numb
But being afraid slowly drains
the life right out of you
until all that is left
is something small
Nobody can see in
It's still better than the nothingness

Feeling angry
is bigger and better than being afraid
But being angry is exhausting and scares the chickens
But at least you feel you are alive
at least something is happening
at least it's a start
Even if it spills out
at least people know you're there

And somewhere after numb
somewhere between the fear and the dread
through the fury and the madness
A real life begins

Courage to move out of the numbness
ignoring the sirens, the alarm bells
the signposts warning of danger

Courage to be scared
Courage to grow big enough
to hold the rage

Courage to forgive

Courage to take your life
back from the past

Claiming
This is now
This is mine

NO MATTER

Having an abusive childhood
a life interrupted
is much like any other chronic condition
We learn to live with it
We learn to manage it
But we never truly recover

No matter how hard we try
no matter how much work we do
no matter who we tell
The stories still remain

No matter who we ask
no matter how many books we read
how many therapists we see
Nothing can save us

No matter how far we run
how many bids for freedom
no matter how many plans we make
There is no escape

No matter how many deals we make
how much we numb or pretend
no matter where we hide
The shadows still chase us

No matter how much noise we make
how much we protest
no matter who we tell
no matter which secrets we keep
The ghosts haunt us

No matter who we become
how much we build
how successful we are
That scared, mistrustful child

can still find us in our quiet

We have to work more
run faster, try harder
to find that place
where most others simply start

There is no tolerable way to explain
Nobody sees

So we hide, we pretend, we struggle
And we fail

My attitude had always been that the past is the past and that's where it should stay. It couldn't be changed and bringing this stuff up only made me feel horrid, so I didn't. The trapdoor to my childhood basement was bolted shut and heavily guarded. Nothing got in, nothing got out.

Then, out of the blue, my mother mentioned that my cousin - the daughter of the abusing uncle - had written a book called *Daddy's Little Favourite,* about her father sexually abusing her. #Metoo.

The trapdoor was blown to pieces. The stories, the memories, the emotions, the fear, the confusion of my childhood came crawling out of the hole and I was powerless to stop it. The memories kept creeping out of that dark basement into the light, right there in the middle of my living room.

I knew exactly why she had chosen that name for the book. He used to say the same thing to me, "You are my little favourite".

Within a month, I'm visiting said cousin, keeping her company through many boring hours of dialysis. I hardly had to say anything. Just, "Mum told me you're writing a book…" - "He got to you too, didn't he?" My answer, of course, was, "Yes". And then she gave me the best advice I have ever had in regards to my abusive past. "Take it from me, do anything, everything you can to get over this shit. Everything. Or you will end up like this. And my sister, she didn't die from being an alcoholic, you know, she died from a broken heart. A broken spirit. Broken".

"So", I asked, "you reckon this kidney problem is because of the abuse". She answered, "No. That's not what I'm saying. It's the *not* dealing with the abuse that made me sick". A year or so later, she also died.

Both sisters were in their 40s.

We are not responsible for what was done to us as children, but we are responsible for the debris left behind. Only we can do the work, get the help, make the choices that move us towards healing. We have to do that work, while battling with all the voices screaming inside - *it's not fair, how come they get away with it, they don't have to do anything, it's not fair.*

The voices are right. It's not fair.

The abusers just get on with their lives, while we have to put in the time, energy, and money (healing ain't cheap). We can kick and shout and stubbornly pout and object, but nothing changes the fact that only we can do what needs to be done.

But often we stay stuck struggling to keep that trapdoor tightly shut. We waste energy on blaming and shaming along with other tactics - anything to postpone doing the work we actually need to do.

Even now, after all these years, this stuff can still jump out and bite me. And yes, I still resist and sulk and complain - *not again, no, I've done enough, it's not my fault, why me, it's not fair, I've had enough.*

In the end, the right voices get through all the clamour and remind me once again - "It's not your fault, but it is your responsibility to do whatever it takes. Now get on with it". Once again, it's hard, and once again, I come out the other end a little bit more intact than I was before.

I lost my childhood to abuse. I misplaced my teenagehood by pretending, protecting, feeling inadequate and flawed. I wasted many of my middle years in trying too hard, overcompensating - still feeling inadequate but not quite so flawed.

Now, I've finally made friends with my past and learnt to manage the symptoms. I'll be buggered if I will lose the rest of my life to regret. I am determined to put everything I know into practice. I have nothing to lose.

I know I have said this before, but it is worth repeating, because taking responsibility without shame is the critical first step. We are not to blame for what happened to us when we are young. We are, however, responsible for cleaning up the debris inside us.

To forgive doesn't erase the past and the present can't diminish what has happened. It can never be a clean slate, no matter what the new-age gurus try to tell us. It's about constantly reminding ourselves that it is only a shadow - a memory - it can't hurt us anymore. We can't change the past, but we can save the rest of our lives.

I recently read a book called *Choice* by Edith Eger. Her story is huge; she survived the Warsaw ghetto, Auschwitz, and the long march. The book is harrowing, humbling, truly inspirational. It left me thinking that my life had been a doddle, and that it was time to pull my socks up and just get on with it.

Until I realised that she didn't write her book to prove that her story was worse than mine or anyone else's. Quite the opposite. She wrote the book to help and encourage us all to choose to open the trap door and do whatever it takes, regardless of our particular story.

Whether we like it or not, we carefully carry our stories with us. I've had the privilege of working intimately with people for years, and I have witnessed their many stories and histories. The rule of thumb is, that if what happened then still impacts our life now, chances are you've got some work to do.

We have the right to deal with our pasts without feeling that we will be judged as overreacting or being self absorbed. It's got nothing to do with anyone else but us. We must do the hard work of changing for our own sake - nothing to do with who hurt us.

We can forgive without forgetting. We can heal without invalidating what happened. And we can *choose* how we live our present and how we define our future, irrespective of the past. That's why Edith Eger called her book *Choice.*

My biggest frustration is how long it takes. Recovering from an interrupted childhood can take a lifetime.

OUR PAST MUST STILL BE MET

(forgiving)

RUNNING AWAY
IT WAS DONE

RUNNING AWAY

We can catch the bus, the train, the plane
as we try and leave our old self behind

But it gets there before us
waiting on the platform
the runway, the doorstep

We can run away
around the corner
to the other side of the world

But our past must still be met
We still need to admit
attend and allow

And then the forgiving

IT WAS DONE

I don't know where it starts. Did the story start when I was sexually abused as a child? Did it start when I finally began to confront my past? Did the story start when I made a formal complaint to the police, or when he was charged, or when the court case started? Or did it start when I was sitting in front of him at the High Court?

I had been fully prepped and prepared for the trial. I was ready to go to court to find justice for the 5, 6, 7, 8, 9 year old me. My lawyer, the crown prosecutor, was popping in and out of the tiny room I had been assigned at the court, explaining to me what was happening. He seemed more nervous than me - this was a big story, there were TV cameras and radio reporters outside. Whereas I'd had most of my life to get prepared.

There were delays and more delays. Then the lawyer triumphantly told us that my uncle was prepared to change his plea to guilty, and that we needed to negotiate the terms.

For me, the terms were simple. I knew exactly what I wanted. A face-to-face meeting. From the lawyer's vigorous head shaking, you'd have thought I'd asked to meet the Pope. "Impossible", he told me, "impossible", and he wasn't even going to ask, because apparently it was impossible.

I really didn't care whether he went to prison or not. What I wanted was to be heard. For there to be an ending. Healing. Punishment would give me none of these things.

Next thing I knew, we were in the courtroom in front of the judge. Here was my chance, so I spoke up and asked for the one thing I had always wanted. A meeting. A reckoning. For him to know the impact of what he had done to all of us - as he had abused more than just me. The judge said yes and set a time for the next afternoon.

Now it was my time to get nervous. A brain-numbing, cold-sweating, heart-racing, stomach-churning nervous. I had wanted this moment for as long as I could remember, and now couldn't find what I wanted to say. I numbed my way through the rest of the day and evening. It wasn't until bedtime that my brain kicked into gear and I spent most of the night walking the streets, remembering what I wanted to say and why.

So there we all were, sitting in the High Court, the facilitator laying down the ground rules and me just looking at the uncle. Not with hate or loathing, but with intense curiosity. Who was this man, now in his early eighties, who had impacted so much of my life?

I started by giving him a photo of me at five years old in his backyard with my cousins - his daughters. He said he didn't know who I was, so I told him my parents' names and my name, and told him that he had sexually abused me in the school holidays when we'd come to stay.

He looked at me. I looked at him. A show-down of sorts. I wasn't scared or intimidated, and he knew it. He nodded in recognition and hung his head. I started by telling him that I was not there to insult him, but to find peace for myself. I was there because I didn't want what he'd done to me to keep impacting my life now.

I continued speaking. I told him that I was also there for the others who I knew he'd abused. Then I told him all the ways that his abuse had damaged me. What it had taken for me to be whole enough, to be functional enough, to be sitting in front of him right now. How much time, how much money, how much effort, how much pain it had taken. I looked at him as I spoke. He looked up at me every now and then, but mostly he just looked down at the photo I'd left in front of him. He seemed stunned. No emotion, no words - nothing. If he had cried or emoted or spoken, I wouldn't have believed him when he finally said, "How could you ever forgive me?"

I didn't answer that question, just asked him to make a public statement urging other men like him to come forward to face what they had done. To get help. To give the abused a chance to be heard. He nodded his head. I asked the facilitator if I could shake my uncle's hand. We both stood and I shook his hand, thanking him for listening. It was only then that I became aware of the others in the room: the policewoman who had supported me from day one, the court and prison guards, the facilitator. There was a fragile quiet and a few moist eyes. Even his lawyer came around the table to greet me.

It was done. He was going to prison. But most importantly, I had been heard. Not just by him, but by the authorities who had failed to protect me when I was small. They had seen me now. I was content.

A short while later, I began to feel something else. The contentment was spreading. I felt an openness in my chest, a tenderness in my heart. It was like a gentle breeze shifting through my body. I felt lighter and taller. There were no words left trapped inside me.

In this soft silence, I didn't need anything. It lasted for days. So that others wouldn't worry, I told them that I was tired. But in reality, I was blissful and simply didn't want to be disturbed.

It took me some time to have words for what I was experiencing. Forgiveness had happened. That wee, scared and fragile girl inside me had been given the attention she needed. Forgiveness had taken the place of mistrust and fear. I felt blessed.

WONDERING AT THE WONDERS

(accepting)

UNCONCERNED
THIS SMALL WORLD IS ENOUGH
THE FINAL INJUSTICE
IT DOESN'T MATTER
YOU HOWEVER
MY ONLY PROMISE
FROM MY VIEW OF THE WORLD
SOME KIND OF MURKY GREY

UNCONCERNED

I think the trees are happy with their view
taking their growing time
Arching sideways with the steady wind
Satisfied with their place in the forest
the orchard, or at the bottom of my garden

The river changes course
after long and fierce consultation
with the droughts and the storms

The weeds, the flower buds, my vegetables
grow together and apart
win their place or lose

Seeds move on the breeze
the insides of birds
on the edge of my skirt

Or not

THIS SMALL WORLD IS ENOUGH

A dusk walk along the still wild shore
after days of storm
And these shaky isles
have been rocking and quaking too

On one side of the road, the houses are finishing their day
on the other, the waves are tumbling
head-first into the shore
The day is over but the night has not yet taken charge
The colours have faded
but the moving and the shapes are still sharp and keen

The lone evening star has arrived
between the folds of corrugated cloud
Nobody - nothing - owns this time
It is the witching hour when the
incurably curious cats appear from nowhere

It's at times like this that I almost believe
in ghosts and goblins, fairies and angels
Worldly things cannot find me
I no longer care about decisions, about Donald
about earthquakes or the floods

The eerie air I breathe is more alive
A duet of day and night sounds reach my ears
and my body feels strangely more my own
I find a fullness in my unfolding heart
even the other twilight walkers feel like kin

I savour the majesty more than the madness
happy with my place in the shambles of living

This small world is enough for me
At least until morning

THE FINAL INJUSTICE

I am not afraid of dying
Not yet anyway

I am however
troubled by thoughts
of missing out
All those many things
that will dare to happen
without me

The final injustice
Life going on
without me

IT DOESN'T MATTER

It doesn't matter
if I do or if I don't
if I stop or keep going
if I stay or if I go

There is no such thing
as a destined destination
a single purposeful purpose

All there is
is experience
This choice leads to these experiences
that choice leads to those experiences

It really doesn't matter

YOU HOWEVER

Not you
You've always been brave enough
to be your same self
no matter who is in the room

Not me
I often feel unacceptable
so offer up subtly modified versions of myself
in the hope of keeping safe

You however
delight in the solitary me
the me that hangs around
when I am on my own

MY ONLY PROMISE

I am willing
That is my only promise

The only promise to you
the only promise to life

This oath to myself
Less resistance
more willingness

That is my only promise

FROM MY VIEW OF THE WORLD

If I lived in a world of one
everything would make sense
to me

But I live in a world
with all of you
Believing in the rightness
of my own view
and the likely delusion of yours

Crammed in closer and closer
connected yet disconnected
constantly merging, colliding
acting, interacting, reacting

Fortified behind my own view
refusing to acknowledge yours

SOME KIND OF MURKY GREY

Whenever I desperately want things to be black and white, I usually end up with some kind of murky grey. Right and wrong tend to merge into rightish and wrongish.

What makes a man into a sexual predator? Was he born like that, or did something happen to him? Or both?

People's stories are complicated. People are complicated. What I know of my abusing uncle is hearsay and patchy at best. The more I understand of him and his life, the harder it is to keep it black and white.

He was born in 1925 and brought up in an orphanage. I don't know from what age or why. This was the Depression, and life was hard and those places were harsh and unloving. As was the custom back then, he was fostered out onto multiple farms at a young age. My guess, is that this was actually more about cheap/free labour than providing him with a home.

He married young, had two daughters, and went away to WWII. The story goes that at the end of the war he arrived home, his wife met him at the docks, handed him his two children and said "I'm leaving you". This may simply be a made up story and there's no way of knowing.

He then married my mother's sister, had four more children, umpired softball, taught gymnastics, ran a rural store, sold insurance… and sexually abused an indeterminate number of people. Men, women, and children. He was charismatic, street-smart, and dangerous.

Years ago, I was sitting around a table having breakfast with a group of people. Someone was reading an article about a woman who had tied her children to the clothesline while she went out to work. Justifiably, people were decrying her actions. I too was appalled, but also felt a slight disquiet.

As an adult I have never really been tested. Never been hungry, broke, sleep-deprived, ill, unsupported, alone or under resourced. I would like to think that, if tested, I would always do the right things. But I've never been up against it, so I really don't know.

Privilege is a kind mirror. Who knows what happened to this young mother, or to my uncle? Yes, they had choices - we all do. They made wrong ones. Some hurt and damaged people go on to hurt others, while some don't.

Either could have been me. Or not?

SUCH A TREAT

(gratitude)

SUCH A TREAT
HOW MANY CHANCES
DYING OF GRATITUDE

SUCH A TREAT

A body alive
with sensation
Hands to hold
legs to dance
hunger to feed
eyes to explore
skin to feel

A heart to do
all the wondrous things
that only hearts can do

A mind so peculiar, so private as to
contemplate anything and everything

All of this
for the whole of my life

A world indulgent with play

HOW MANY CHANCES

If I have not been enchanted
by one thing
in this long day

Then maybe I am too ungrateful
too full of entitlement
to deserve another

DYING OF GRATITUDE

When I allow myself to feel the wonder of living, the emotion that floods through me is gratitude. Then I so quickly fall into the well of forgetting - too busy, too distracted. Taking for granted what is good in my life. Blinded by privilege.

We were in the company of a man who was a quadriplegic. He had already astounded me with the joy he found in living, and his appreciation for all the gifts of life. We were all sitting in his garden on an overcast winter's day and he went quiet. The sun had just come out, and after a while, he asked us if we could feel the gorgeous warmth of the sun on our faces. His childlike appreciation touched me, and I have never forgotten.

He brought the world to my attention. He was right. The sun on my face did indeed feel glorious. So did the grass under my feet, the warmth of my friend's hand on my arm, and the coolness of the glass in my hand. And that was just noticing touch and temperature. There was also smell and taste and feeling and thoughts and sound and ...

I was reminded again, when an elderly friend came to live with us for the last month of her life. It was a pleasure and an honour to care for and support her, as she consciously prepared herself to die. During the process of her dying, she spoke often of feeling overwhelmed with gratitude. "I am dying of gratitude" was a sentiment she frequently expressed.

This took my interest, and I asked her if she was feeling gratitude for the life she had lived. She replied no, it was gratitude for her life at this present moment. Knowing she was about to die had focused her on living each moment. Her final comment was that this experience of living fully now left nothing but a vast and overwhelming feeling of gratitude.

I watched her grow more beautiful each day. I concluded that the feeling and expression of gratitude is the most exquisite beauty treatment. At eighty nine years of age, and within days of her death, she looked like an angel.

KNOWING MY BELONGING BY HEART

(belonging)

AOTEAROA
A DAILY RITUAL
OVER AND OVER
NOT EVEN A SANDCASTLE
LONGING TO BELONG

AOTEAROA

She rose from of her mother's molten core
born through a salty embryonic fluid
into a great birthing sea

Lapping waves nursed her body
long winds kissed her flushed cheeks
wandering rivers quenched her parched lips
Ecstatic birdsong proclaiming her arrival
here in these southern oceans
far away from the conforming crowds

Down here with space to grow her wild heart
she formed her fearless mountains
With reverence she planted her trees and ferns
With innocence her beauty overflowed
and with generosity she welcomed all her people

I am in love with this land
deeply honoured to belong to these people
On these sacred islands I claim my place

Enthralled and enchanted as I watch us grow
Sometimes shy and self-conscious
daring and brave

Standing here before a curious world

A DAILY RITUAL

Writers and artists often talk
of walks with the trees or along the shore
This daily ritual

Even if it means striding out
between downpours of winter rain
squalls of equinoctial wind
or strolling through the evening softness
after the heat of a summer day

They know all the shades
of the seasons and the weather
Intimately acquainted with each private landscape
Familiar with the drifting sounds
of waves on the rocks on each and any tide

A confidant to the birds and the people nearby
they feel deeply the changes
the comings and the goings

They know these places of belonging by heart
And from this intimate knowing
they are reminded each day
to go back home and create

OVER AND OVER

Over and over
the same reply

Have I done well
Am I possibly loved
And still
it's over and over
the same reply

Even when I don't believe the answer
Over and over
it's the same reply

Until my body, the sun, the earth
become the answer
my timetable, my guide
Echoing over and over
that same reply

The smile, that look, those words
all tell me the same story
repeating over and over
that same reply

Intimacy comes with each ebb
saturated, yours and mine
and the tides

Over and over
the same reply

NOT EVEN A SANDCASTLE

I want to stand on the beach
and see this landscape as it once was

No tall neat piles of stones
built for some spiritual effect

No moving of the long-bleached driftwood
into beach huts along the shore
Not even a sandcastle

I can ignore the dark sandy roads
and the tracks down to the beach
The holiday homes laden with summer memories
I can even block out the hungry picnic tables

I want to stand on the sand
look out and pretend that this
is nature as it was
Naked
Before we covered it
with a myriad of modifications

I want to stand on the shore
and see only the sand, the waves
the rocks, the seaweed, the sea
the seabirds

A landscape bare of us

LONGING TO BELONG

Only one of my parents was born in New Zealand. All four of my grandparents were born in different countries and none were born here. But I was.

I was in my early teens when I heard Māori activists talking about being a displaced people. I understand the history and I agree.

I also feel that I am dispossessed in a different way. None of my ancestors willingly chose to leave their homeland. My father's family comes from Tasmania. They were not the ruling class, so you can imagine their history. Others of my ancestors arrived here from desperation. I come from a long line of working poor. I doubt they knew about the consequences of immigration and colonisation. They took great risks in the hope of a better, or at least tolerable life.

So that leaves me here, born to this land but not tangata whenua. Growing up in suburbia, I don't have a river or a mountain to anchor me, or call me home. I can't look back to where my ancestors came from, because I am made up of a mishmash of disenfranchised people from many different places. No heritage, no cultural roots, nothing but my birth ties me to the land.

Because I am white and middle class, it's often assumed that I belong to the popular culture of contemporary New Zealand. But I don't. I don't follow sport - not even rugby. I don't follow mainstream media or entertainment. I'm out of step with mainstream culture. I don't like fish and chips, and even ANZAC day doesn't fill me with nationalist pride.

Yes, my white middle-classness gives me privileges which I have enjoyed all my life. But it doesn't give me belonging. That deep, deep knowing that I have a right to belong to this place. I do feel it sometimes, when I hear ruru calling in the night, see a valley full of tree ferns, or walk along a wild windy coast. Other times, that longing to belong is still there.

HOLDING MY OWN HAND

(being alone)

THIS GIVEN TIME
I SLEPT WITH MYSELF LAST NIGHT
MAKING BAD DEALS
I WANT MY HEART BACK
WHEN I STOP INTERRUPTING MYSELF
SITTING ON THE DOORSTEP
ME IN THE MIDDLE

THIS GIVEN TIME

I don't arrive in places like this very often
This given time

Time alone
not rushing through

Delight in the honesty of my own style
nothing sidelined
Me in the middle
in the corners, in the garden, on the couch
through the door, in the mirror

My loving arms around my life
sweet words whispered to my own goodnights

I don't arrive in places like this very often
This given time

Time alone

I SLEPT WITH MYSELF LAST NIGHT

I slept with myself last night
arms and legs outstretched
touching the sides of my own silence

Without fiction or fancy
I was only a little afraid
of the solitary darkness

Tonight I may again arch slightly
longing towards some ghostly
or imagined someone

Or I may sleep well with myself
curled up in the wonder and comfort
of my own heartbeat
Lying in my own bed
with my own body
my own thoughts

In this
my own life

MAKING BAD DEALS

Making bad deals
as I trade myself for approval

Letting my need for love
override my self-respect
Trading my integrity for love

I'm putting a sign on my heart
'Not for Sale or Lease'
to remind myself
that my heart is to be shared

Never to be traded

I WANT MY HEART BACK

I want my heart back

Having given it away
in some pointless bargain
I have abandoned myself

Distraught
I have tried to fill this empty heart space
with any poor substitute

I want my heart
warm and full inside

Then it can overflow
to share with another

WHEN I STOP INTERRUPTING MYSELF

To no longer be afraid of my own thoughts
to stop spooking myself
Scaring myself breathless
with doubt and self-judgement
To stop pushing myself around
with threats or worse

To allow soft space for silence
To be a kind and thoughtful host to the quiet
To stop interrupting myself

To spend enough kind-time with myself
so that we can become
fast friends

SITTING ON THE DOORSTEP

It is useless
to go out in search of love
if on return
all the windows and doors
are still bolted shut

Stay home and do the work
until the windows and doors
swing freely on their hinges

Clear the garden path
make some tea
sit on the doorstep
and wait

ME IN THE MIDDLE

I was fifty before I truly lived on my own. I'd lived in my family home, then in shared flats, then married, married with children, married without children, not married with housemates and then, finally, alone.

It happened when I moved to a new city and into a small one-bedroom basement flat. It was cosy and I felt safe. I had a desk, a bed, a couch, and nothing much else to identify with or to confine me.

Coming home from work on that very first evening, I was like a dog not knowing where to sit. I went around and around the room in smaller and smaller circles until I finally plonked myself down in the middle of the room. I had no idea what to do with myself. For as long as I could remember, I would decide what I was going to do based on what the people around me need, or what needed to be done.

Here I was with no thing and no one needing me. I didn't have any idea of what to do with myself, and just sat dog-like in the middle of the room looking lost. My mind was blank, and I honestly did not know what I wanted.

I took my aimlessness for a walk up the hill, came home, ate some food, then found myself back in the middle of the floor dumbfounded. The next day was much the same. I got home, automatically went for a walk up the hill, and had some dinner. At least I had that part sorted. Then it was back to sitting in the middle of the room, my mind blank.

On the first weekend, I woke up, had breakfast, cleaned and tidied, did the washing - and it was only 9.30 in the morning. I still had the whole weekend left. Not knowing what to do, I did nothing but walk, eat, and read.

It was a few weeks before I noticed the change. I was walking up the path to my home, and felt this excitement in my belly, accompanied by the in-my-head-words "tonight, dear Jane, you have the whole evening to yourself - you can do whatever you want".

By the next day, walking up the path had turned into this delicious feeling of freedom. I still didn't need to know what to do, but I did know that I could do whatever I wanted. No 'shoulds' or 'have-tos'. My now daily walk up the hill suddenly felt like an escape. Eating whatever I wanted, whenever I wanted - or not - became an act of claimed sovereignty. Sewing, writing, gardening, all became symbols of a recovered independence. It kept getting better.

With time and attention, I recognised my own rhythms. It was a revelation to live in my own flow. To live my own style. It's all very well to have the option to choose, but another thing altogether to know what to choose.

Happily living with now-husband, it is important for me to compromise and make room for his tastes and his rhythms. But now, knowing my starting place, I can negotiate without giving myself away.

Not having had this sense of self for much of my life, and having worked so hard to find it, I don't give up easily.

RECOGNISING EACH OTHER

(love)

LOVE TAKES ITS TIME
STAYING CLOSE ENOUGH
I SIMPLY FORGET
WAIT MY DARLING CHILDREN
I HAD ALWAYS KNOWN
BREADCRUMB TRAILS
BELIEVING WE ARE LOVED

LOVE TAKES ITS TIME

True love can only ever come slowly
No matter how much we want
to hurry through to safe ground

It takes time to find
the securing glue of shared memories
of enough living together
to join two lives

No matter how fast we want love
to knit us together
The beginning is always precarious
as we slowly twist the threads
into something that can withstand
the yanks, the wear, loose ends
without unravelling

We can't push love any faster
than the crafty fingers of time
can weave us together

STAYING CLOSE ENOUGH

He smells of good things
I knew it
as soon as we stood close enough

Something earthy
a musk that is almost musty
Reminds me of two-day-old
damp mown grass left in rows
on the old school playing field

That smell of the first spring dig
of my waking garden
Summer rain in the forest
the mulch of autumn leaves
smoky winter evening walks

This man
smelling of all things good
Still stays close enough

I SIMPLY FORGET

Before you
my real life was always being alone

Even with the ones I truly love
I'm still being mother, companion, advisor
Even if just a little

After the busyness, after the activity
after the conversation, after the experience
I would find myself again
in my solitude
With nobody, nothing
to second guess

But with you
I simply forget
Even when you are in the room
even when you are lying next to me
even when we are holding hands
even in the kiss
even when I doubt

With you
I simply forget

WAIT MY DARLING CHILDREN

When you marry Safety and Security
the safe haven inevitably becomes a trap
Or the endless boredom
means you eventually make
a tedious escape

When you marry Passion
You're dizzy and giddy
swinging from ecstasy to despair
Overcome with exhaustion
as you crawl away in embarrassed defeat

When you marry Money and Status
You shamefully dislike yourself
but snobbishly despise them more
Finally you rebel or are expelled
taking away as much collateral as you can carry

When you marry Duty
you are crushed under the obligation
as you disappear into dulled conformity
Or live out your life-sentence
spiting, spitting, swiping
resenting

When you marry Habit
laziness means you forget to choose
Your life waltzes past
in a monotonous but adequate blur
and you never quite get around to leaving

So wait my darling children
Wait until being with them brings out
what you most like about yourself
When resolving conflict
is a mutual discovery

When they make you laugh
and you don’t have to try so hard

I HAD ALWAYS KNOWN

Deep down
I had always known
my Love would come

But in my impatience
I agreed too soon
and said yes to someone else's loving
Or maybe I was just too scared to wait

Then again
if we had met back then
would we have recognised each other
could our younger selves have known

Now
you are here
My Love has come

BREADCRUMB TRAILS

Already

Already I have let myself
go beyond any place
I have ever allowed my heart
to venture before

I have wandered so far
into love's enchanted forest
that I have forgotten to be scared
of the witches, the bad wolves
and all the other traps
set for an innocent heart

The old love stories tell me
there may be no way back
The navigation star
is lost on a clouded night
The breadcrumb trails
have all been eaten

I'd heard about these hidden doors
that lead us into forgotten gardens
Until we get so lost
that we never want to be found again

We had known Helen for many years. She was 89 by the time she came to live with us. Her diagnosis was terminal, and it made sense for her to be with us during the last weeks or months of her life. We had plenty of space for her friends and family to visit or stay.

Her Dutch directness often came across as sharp, and I had been at the end of a few pointed comments over the years. She could be caring and caustic in the same breath. She had a clever, curious mind and an artist's temperament, which makes sense, as she was, among other things, an artist.

Helen was an exceptional woman, but she wouldn't have agreed with that statement. People, me included, found her inspirational. She had provided a safe house for Jewish children during the war. She couldn't understand what all the fuss was about, as in her mind she had 'just done the right thing'. Once the word got out that she was dying, the phone rang red hot from Israel as those now-grown children rang to say thank you one last time.

After she had organised what would happen to all her possessions, she moved on to organising her funeral. It was actually fun helping her decide what she wanted. She even had me take photos of her in different outfits while she lay in dead pose - flat on her back, eyes closed, arms crossed over her chest. Having decided what she was going to wear, she gave me strict instructions on how to do her hair.

We were talking about what she wanted to be written on her memorial card when she started to get grumpy. She was not happy. "I've been doing all this planning. All my favourite people are going to be there and I won't. Well, I will, but I'll be dead. They will say nice things about me - they always do at funerals - and I won't get to hear them".

The idea was floated that we have a pre-funeral funeral for her. We could hold it right here in our big yoga teaching room, and should do it as soon as possible, before she popped her clogs. So it was decided, and so it happened.

The day came and the people started arriving. She was near dying, so we had to manage her energy levels. Then-husband took the people out into the front garden and I stayed with Helen. We could hear lots of commotion and hilarity as people arrived, and Helen insisted that I go find out what was happening. I came back with the news that more people were arriving than we had invited. Seems word had got out. "You're famous Helen. You're famous and you're loved. And guess what, there is a big surprise on it's way from Sydney". Her greatly loved godson was coming to say goodbye.

She went very quiet, looking down at a piece of paper she had beside her. She tapped it and fiddled with the corners, and then she read me the email. It was from a Buddhist teacher who was an old friend of hers. I don't remember the exact words, but the gist was: *Stay present through the whole process of dying, don't miss anything. Make dying your meditation, breath it all in, until your last breath.*

"I am loved", was all she said, with tears running down her face. "Finally I believe it, finally I can let it in. I am loved". She looked like an angel, soft, still, translucent and utterly beautiful. Loving is hard I thought, but believing we are loved is even harder.

Then we heard the chatter of people coming down the hall. When they entered the room however, they went silent. They filed by her one at a time - tears, kisses, hand-holding, hands held up in prayer, a few hushed words. The love poured out and Helen took it all in. The room was full of people and emotion. Her Buddhist friends chanted and her dear Christian friend said a prayer. People told stories and we learnt more about what she had given - each of us with our own Helen story. There was wordless wailing from a much younger woman who was also dying. There was space for that too.

She continued by saying "If there aren't disagreements in a marriage, then someone is a doormat". Her final piece of wisdom was "Never take offence, dear. We are all just doing the best we can, and nobody means to hurt the ones they love. Just stay open and keep doing your best. That's the only way I know to keep the loving alive".

NEVER TO BE FOUND AGAIN

(committing)

PUSHING AGAINST EACH OTHER
WAKE ME LIKE THIS
EVEN THOUGH YOU HAVE GONE
I GIVE UP
MAKING IT LAST

PUSHING AGAINST EACH OTHER

When our views don't like each other
and we both want our own way
When I push
please push back
Not so hard
that I fall over, flattened
Just hard enough
that I know where you stand

Don't give in either
leaving me in mid-air
I need to know
you are firmly there

As we push against each other
as we rock between our positions
we form a stable yet swaying base

Knowing where the other stands
we can trust in our differences

WAKE ME LIKE THIS

When I irritate you
when I do those things
that hurt
that undermine

Remember that I am asleep
dead to the world of those around me
stumbling and lost
somewhere old and troubled

Be kind and rouse me gently
as I am charging about
in an old and murky dream
and I have forgotten to be kind to you

Wake me like this
as you ease me back through
these hard and unforgiving walls
Bring me back to my real and loving life

And forgive me
as I may fall asleep again

EVEN THOUGH YOU HAVE GONE

I still know you
even though you are no longer here
You are still my beloved, my friend
even were I to commit to another

I still have a relationship with you
the things I still show you
our conversations inside my head
the continuing stories from our shared past

What was once companionship between two
has become my sacred internal communion

I GIVE UP

I have changed my mind

You don't have to completely understand me
You don't have to know
how to give me everything I need

In the struggle to get your full agreement
everything becomes disagreeable

Therefore
I give up
I give in

I asked a woman who had been married for sixty-two years if the marriage was good. She said yes. So I asked her the obvious question, "How do you do it; how do you keep the relationship alive?" She answered that it had taken a long time to work out.

For the first ten years she thought that once they had sorted out their differences, all would be sweet. After twenty years, she was disappointed and resentful that they hadn't. It took her another five years to realise that they would never sort out their differences, but that wasn't the point.

She told me that marriage is about learning how to disagree without hurting or withdrawing from each other. It is about being able to lovingly communicate your needs to the other, while being open to hearing the needs of the other. Even when these needs are in conflict.

In fact, that very morning they'd had an argument about which colour to paint the cupboards. They decided to hold off until the next day and, meanwhile, she would go get some more paint charts. It wasn't about compromising or trying to convince the other to change their mind. It was about staying with the negotiation until they found a resolution they would both be happy *enough* with.

She continued by saying "If there aren't disagreements in a marriage, then someone is a doormat". Her final piece of wisdom was "Never take offence, dear. We are all just doing the best we can, and nobody means to hurt the ones they love. Just stay open and keep doing your best. That's the only way I know to keep the loving alive".

I spent years working with couples in trouble. If they walked in the door and they were still fighting and sniping, then I knew there was hope. If they walked in calm and distant, I knew it was going to be a hard slog.

The opposite of love is not hate. It is indifference.

BANGING INTO EACH OTHER

(communicating)

THIS PERFECT DISCONNECT
IN TOO MANY WORDS
THE EMOTIONAL FILING CABINET
NOT JUST THEM
JUST FOR LISTENING
STORIES
A WEE TASTE
WHEN I AM IN PAIN
I WILL NOT ASK
SHOW ME

THIS PERFECT DISCONNECT

We measure ourselves by our intent
knowing we mean no harm

We measure others by their impact
the harm they are causing us

This perfect disconnect
this dividing rift
means we drift even further apart

Can we bear to hear
the impact we have on others
irrespective of our intent
Holding quietly our dearly held
excuses and explanations

Can we listen to their intent
no matter how hurt
or wronged we may feel

Can we judge others
as we judge ourselves

Can we connect this disconnect
by walking across the bridge
between intention and impact

IN TOO MANY WORDS

When words won't work
when they get snarled and snagged
When the meaning gets lost in all the talk
and their definition escapes

That's when we let the silence
of our simply being here
do all that is needed

Hold my hand
as we walk
Put your arms around me
as we meet
Touch my back
so I know I have done well
Stroke my head
when I am ailing
Nod your head
so I know that you know
Rub my cheek
as I wake
Caress me
so I feel your care
Point the way
when I am lost
Hold me tight
when grief takes hold
Smile generously
when I walk through the door
Stand up for me
when I can't do it for myself
but sit down again
when I remember how

Touch me

Quietly

THE EMOTIONAL FILING CABINET

Get off your high horse
Sell off the high moral ground
Decommission the complaints department
Stop trying to balance the books

Empty out the emotional filing cabinet

They didn't get out of bed this morning
simply to get up your nose
Their story about you
sounds just as compelling
as your story about them

Empty out the emotional filing cabinet

NOT JUST THEM

Nobody likes to be made wrong
Not just them
us too

We can't change anyone
by making them wrong
All they will do is push back
or shut down

All we can do
is be kind and clear
Influence how they are with us
by how we are with them

JUST FOR LISTENING

I would like three heads please
One to think with
one to speak with
and another
just for listening

It's tiring trying
to think and talk and listen
with just one head

STORIES

There are two sides to every story
Not just ours

A WEE TASTE

A conversation
is a smorgasbord of ideas
having lunch together

A conversation
is where we have a wee taste
of things we don't already know

A good conversation
is a feast for the mind

WHEN I AM IN PAIN

In this moment
I don't need you to fix me
I don't need your sympathy or your kindly advice
Please don't try to convince me it's not so bad
or pretend that this isn't happening

To do this
leaves me
lonely, angry, invisible, shamed

What I need most
is your acknowledgement
of my pain
of my discomfort

Ask me just one question
What do you need right here
right now

And if I can't answer
simply do something simple for me
Something nurturing
so I feel your care

I WILL NOT ASK

I want you to want to
I don't want to ask

If you really loved me
you would know
If you really loved me
I wouldn't have to ask

I want you to be the adult
and know what I want
And I want to be the child
and not have to ask

I may sulk
I may snipe

But I will not ask

SHOW ME

I took Daughter-Number-One to see where I grew up. We looked at the house, and as we walked along the street I told her stories. *This is where I fell off my bike and took the skin off my knuckles — see, the scar is still there. That's where Mrs Spooner lived, she looked after me whenever I was sick. That's where the Zaniches lived, their whole backyard was a vegetable garden...* and so the stories continued.

When we got to the end of the street, I told her about the place just over there where I would go when I felt most lonely. When I was confused or overcome with feeling and didn't know what else to do. I pointed to the tree, very close to the cliff that overlooked the river, where I would sit and hide so nobody could find me.

"Show me" she said. And there it was, just as it had been 50 years earlier. The tree had grown, but then so had I. We crawled below the bottom branches and sat down. From habit I sat with my knees tucked right up under my chin, making myself as small, as very small, as possible. My darling daughter sat next to me as close as she could, resting her hand on the back of my neck.

Time disappeared, and I drifted back into that intense loneliness, as real in that moment as it had been when I was young. And yet, there was caring right beside me. At the same time, I was both back-there and right-here. The most precious thing was that the loving presence was my own daughter. Proof that I did find my way. A living witness that I would not always feel so lonely. Evidence that I would find my place to belong.

A DEEPER CONVERSATION WITH MYSELF

(appreciation)

WONDERING AT THE WONDERS

I am deeply fascinated by the holes
dug through the pavements and the streets

A reminder that below us is always earth
microbes and history and old roots
There were trees and grasses
creatures and streams and such

Don't get me wrong
I am most grateful
for roads and tap water and plugs and phones
All the privileges that raw-nature does not need

Sometimes
when I look into these open holes
I wonder at the wonders
we have buried and lost

FULLY IN LOVE

Just because I don't believe in a god
doesn't mean that I never meet with the sacred
Just because I don't give credit to a divining hand
doesn't mean I don't experience what I cannot see

I'm fully in love with beauty and kindness
with courage and joy
My awe at sunrise is no less because
I don't believe it is orchestrated
by someone's god

My appreciation of the bounty of life
stands for me
against a backdrop of chance and disorder
Nothing more than what is real
right here, right now

No need to close my eyes
or sit cross legged

All I need is my garden, the beach, the bush
Any quiet, any beauty, any stillness
will bring me to this deeper conversation
with myself

WILBUR WALKING

I walk my neighbour's dog
I don't get Wilbur's fierce loyalty
but I do get his companioned approval

He likes the unleashed beach
where his wild dogness takes over
as he follows every smell
every fast-flying bird
just out of running reach

I trust he knows his limits
He trusts I won't leave him behind

We also walk the nearby bush tracks
Leashed, he has no chance
of chasing the slower birds

I take him for coffee and sometimes a beer
He likes the attention
and in return attends to those
who stop to say a dog-hello

I like to walk my neighbour's dog
Happy to live in a neighbourhood
where we walk each other's dogs
Where we talk to each other
We know each other

ENDLESS HOURS

I remember those times
the corner shop where I bought my milkshakes
roaming the neighbourhood
nobody watching
nobody needing to

Ant trails and summer plums
endless hours playing until after dusk
just enough light to find our way home

Even though my childhood home was hard
it was still full of stretchy time

Now
the hours merge
the days collapse into one another
Time spreads like butter on hot toast
and before I know it
breakfast is done

GRAB YOUR COAT

Grab your coat
we're going out
Now
Somewhere, there, anywhere

Not when the sun is right
or the wind is light
when the floor is swept
or the inbox cleared

Grab your warmest jacket
this earth can't wait one minute longer
No, we don't have time for me to explain
No, it doesn't matter what shoes you wear

When we are facing into the cold spray
our hands dug deep into warm pockets
We'll witness the sea birds
piloted by wild winds
Feel the small pebbles tremble
as the waves hurtle head-first
arguing incessantly with the shore

BARE FEET

Feeling something
other than the inside of my shoes
My tender spring feet
touching the sand and the stones

Out on an early evening walk

This dusk is warm and still
a change after
the constant cold sea winds

Summer is promising her annual visit
soon the sea will be ready
for a breathless dip

I'll stay here a little longer
to wait and welcome
her trusted arrival

I watched her eyes, alive with tears of joy, mourning, and gratitude.

She talked about getting married, about her daughter who had died twenty years before. About turning forty and her delight and gratitude for her work as a midwife. She talked of the hard times with her teenage daughter and the relief as things improved. No matter the topic, her eyes shone with the same quality of gratitude. Even when we planted a tree to commemorate the death of her newborn daughter twenty years earlier, she was still honouring and celebrating.

I had the privilege of holding the space for her and her women friends, as we prepared for her wedding that evening. For all the reasons mentioned, this was a potent time in her life, and she simply wanted to celebrate everything. I was mesmerised as I watched and was shown a most precious lesson. That all of life is a celebration.

My father's death at 82 was a celebration, because he died just as he'd lived. The days leading up to his death were joyful for him. Mostly because he got to do it his way. No doctors, no drugs, no hospital, no fuss. Just him and me.

Hours before he slipped into a coma, he asked me to take him for a walk in his wheelchair up the beautiful valley where I lived. His eyes were alive and shining as he said goodbye to life.

I was married to someone from India, the land of celebration, where any occasion is a reason for festivity. Colour, smell, music, food, clothes, light, prayer, myth, ritual. Anything and everything.

On the other hand, I come from a country of understatement. To celebrate beyond Christmas and birth days is sometimes considered unnecessary or extravagant. But these experiences have changed me. I have become very loose in my celebrating. Any excuse will do.

SHOWING UP EVERYWHERE

(happiness)

KEEPING ME COMPANY
CHECKING I'M HAPPY
SUFFICE
SOAKED THROUGH
EVERY SMALL THING

KEEPING ME COMPANY

This happiness
came from nowhere
Not from this or that or from you

This happiness
just hung around
and kept me company

When my day tried
to busy and bustle me along
this happiness suggested
that I hold on tightly
to her hand

CHECKING I'M HAPPY

He calls to ask
how my morning had been
that darling husband of mine

I tell him everything I have done
but he just wants to know
that I'd enjoyed myself

So I tell him how well
my tasks have gone
But he just wants to know
that I'm happy

SUFFICE

I am ready to abandon the world
Not to die
not unless I have to

But to empty my bags
my mind
my house
of what I thought I wanted

Now
emptied
I'm giving what life
had wanted from me all along

To care for the earth
where I stand
To care for the hearts
given to me in trust

SOAKED THROUGH

I turned happiness away

I tried to explain
about the problems of the world
my own troubles
the angst and the anguish

Happiness persisted
Showing up everywhere
Never listening to a word

Until my resolve it broke
and happiness flooded through
soaking everything

EVERY SMALL THING

I love to sit at my front door. I open the door, move a comfortable chair in line with the sun and keep moving the chair as the sun moves. I know it by heart.

The stillness of my garden, the sounds of my neighbourhood and of the birds. The sun's movement over the northern sky. I know where it dips below the trees in the depths of winter and the slant of the rays as it goes higher in the warmer skies. The shapes of the tree shadows. The cats always claiming the sunniest spot - they too, move with the arc of the sun.

I watch the slow battle between the weeds and my preciously sowed plants. I look with anticipation each spring to see which plants have decided to show up again. Their growing delights me. I make a gift of my compost to help them and give my thanks.

I am in sweet relationship with sitting at my front door. These are the things I love with all my heart. I wouldn't swap them for a trip to Bali, or, as my Nana would say, for all the tea in China. I don't want to be anywhere else or have anything more.

I no longer notice that the door needs painting or the fence needs finishing. I may fix or finish these things on that day when it's what I want to do. The door still does its opening and closing, its hellos and goodbyes. The fence still does its dividing and still forms a canvas for the creeping rose. The front doormat still does its sole cleaning and the door key still helps me feel safe. Every small thing doing what it does.

And now the sun has moved behind the other side of the house and it's time for me to shut the door and turn the chair back. Here I find my cats already sitting close by, in anticipation of my lighting the fire. The distant hills are beginning to soften and fade. The next attraction is the setting sun. The food is ready for my cooking, and soon my beloved will come home.

ACKNOWLEDGEMENTS

Most importantly to my husband Peter, for giving me the space and encouragement to fulfill my lifetime dream of being a writer. Even though it has taken way longer than he -and I - thought.

To my children who always believe in me, even when I don't.

To my close friends, for reading through the many drafts and giving such useful feedback.

Again to Peter for his honest and insightful editing.

To all my friends and clients. Thanks for the support, the teaching, the endless rants, and the love and laughs.

ABOUT THE AUTHOR

Jane lives in Wellington, New Zealand with her husband Peter. She spends her days tending her garden, walking her dog, and writing. She still sometimes works as a mediator, facilitator, and communications coach and presenter.

She has written two other books: *Follow Yourself Home* and *Word Remedies*.

For more information and for book purchases, go to her website: www.wordremedies.co.nz

Alternatively, you can purchase ebooks and physical books directly from Amazon, or other similar platforms.

INDEX OF REMEDY TITLES

and first lines

I

J

K

L

M

N

O

P

Q

R

S

T

U

W

Y

Printed in Great Britain
by Amazon

76749826R00128